Library and Information Service

Library materials must be returned on or before the last due date or fines will be charged at the current rate. Items can be renewed by telephone, email or by visiting the website, letter or personal call unless required by another borrower. For hours of opening and charges see notices displayed in libraries.
Tel: 03333 704700
Email: libraries@lewisham.gov.uk
www.lewisham.gov.uk/libraries

Feb 18

1 2 AUG 2018

SALMON

Words that look like **this** can be found in the glossary on page 24.

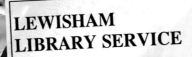

©2018
Book Life
King's Lynn
Norfolk PE30 4LS

ISBN: 978-1-78637-238-3

Written by:
Holly Duhig
Edited by:
Kirsty Holmes
Designed by:
Danielle Jones

A catalogue record for this book
is available from the British Library.

SALMON

WHAT IS A LIFE CYCLE?

All animals, plants and humans go through different stages of their life as they grow and change. This is called a life cycle.

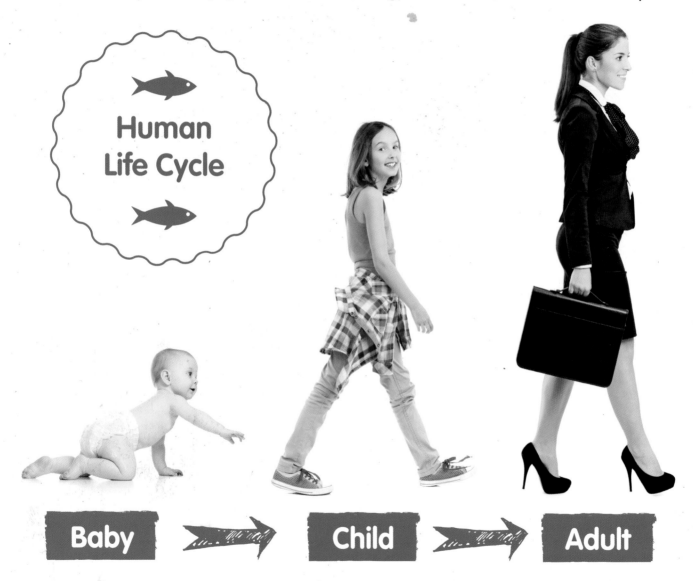

Human
Life Cycle

Baby ➤ **Child** ➤ **Adult**

WHAT IS A SALMON?

A salmon is a type of fish. Most fish live either in **freshwater** or in the sea. Salmon are able to live in both.

Freshwater River

Sea

EGGS

Salmon dig their nests using their tails.

Female salmon lay their eggs in a nest called a redd. They make their nests by digging holes in the gravel which covers the riverbed.

Salmon eggs are small and orange, and are hidden in between the gravel. This hides them from **predators**, like birds or other fish.

ALEVINS

After about six weeks, the eggs hatch. Newly-hatched salmon are called alevins. They still have their egg's **yolk** attached to them, which they eat for **nutrients**.

Alevin

Alevins stay in the gravel, feeding off their egg's yolk until they are strong enough to swim around. The yolk lasts for about 30 days.

FRY

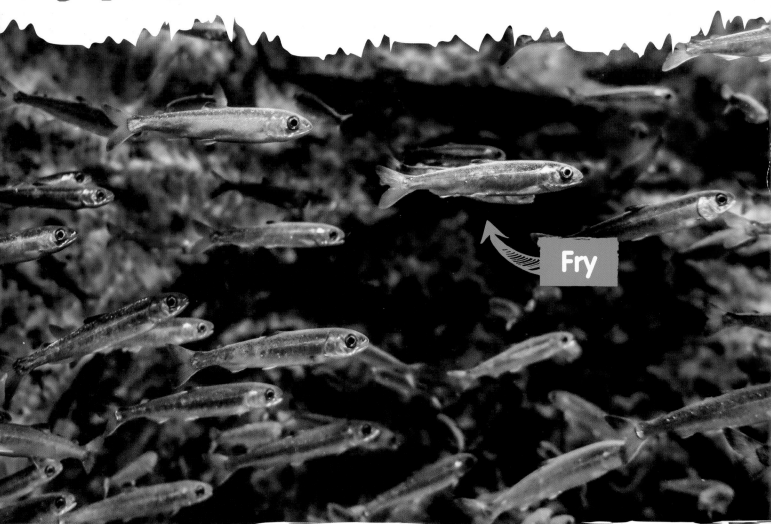

Fry

Once alevins have eaten all their yolk and grown bigger, they become tiny fish, called fry. The fry swim up through the gravel and start to look for food.

Fry swim to the surface of the water and take a big gulp of air. This fills up their **swim bladder,** which allows them to swim without floating or sinking.

CHANGING FRY

Parr Marks

Fry develop dark stripes, called parr marks, on their bodies. This helps **camouflage** them against the riverbed so their predators find it harder to spot them.

Fry begin to explore their **surroundings**. They need to remember the river they were born in so they can return as adults to lay their own eggs.

SALMON

This fry is losing its markings and becoming a smolt.

Before fry become adults, they become smolts. When fry become smolts they lose their parr markings and **migrate** towards the ocean.

Smolts' bodies change as they become adults, so that they are able to live in the salty ocean water. Salmon live in the ocean for around two to five years.

Salmon in the Ocean

THE SALMON'S JOURNEY

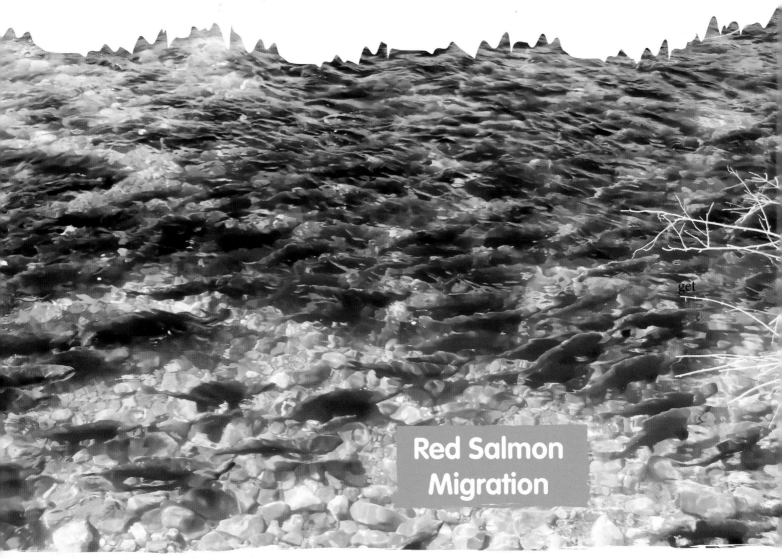

get

Red Salmon
Migration

After this, the salmon migrate back to the rivers they were born in. They travel hundreds of kilometres **upstream**. This migration is called the salmon run.

Travelling upstream often means salmon have to get over rocks and waterfalls. They do this by jumping high in the air.

Salmon can jump over three metres into the air.

FISHY FACTS

No one really knows how salmon are able to find the river they were born in. Some experts think they use their sense of smell or the ocean **currents**.

Salmon are often caught by eagles and grizzly bears as they swim upstream.

WORLD RECORD BREAKERS

World's Biggest Salmon Species

The biggest species of salmon is the chinook salmon. Most chinook salmon are between 61 and 91 centimetres long. They often have red or purple **scales** on their back.

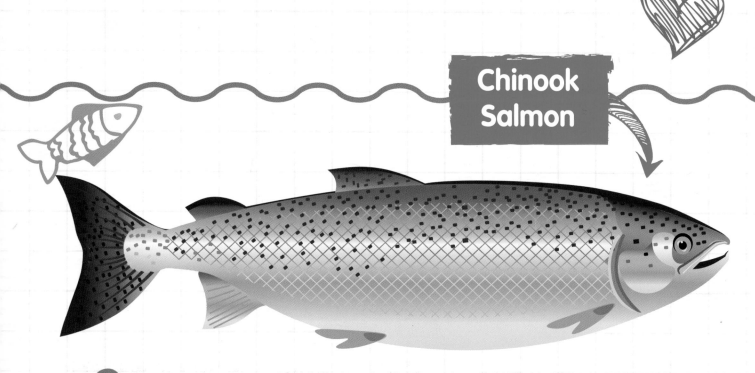

Chinook Salmon

Biggest Salmon Ever Caught

The biggest salmon ever caught was a chinook salmon. It was over 1.5 metres long and weighed 44 kilograms. It was caught on the 17th of May, 1985, in Alaska.

LIFE CYCLE OF A SALMON

1 A female salmon lays her eggs in a redd.

2 The alevins hatch and emerge from the eggs, then become fry.

LIFE CYCLES

The adult salmon return to the river they were born in to lay eggs of their own.

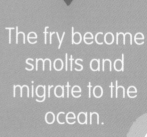

3 The fry become smolts and migrate to the ocean.

4

GET EXPLORING!

Top Tip! Always be careful around water. Make sure you have an adult with you.

Are there any rivers near to where you live? Why not go and see if you can spot any salmon? Are they swimming upstream or downstream?

GLOSSARY

camouflage	when an animal is hard to see because it is the same colour as its habitat
currents	steady flows of water in one direction
freshwater	water that is not salty and doesn't come from the sea
migrate	the seasonal movement of animals from one area to another
nutrients	natural substances that plants and animals need to grow and stay healthy
predators	animals that hunt other animals for food
scales	small circles of thin bone that protect the skin of fish and reptiles
surroundings	the things and conditions around a person or thing
swim bladder	an air–filled sac in the bodies of many fish which is used to control floating and sinking
upstream	against the flow of the current, towards the source of a river
yolk	the nutritious part of an egg

INDEX

PHOTO CREDITS

Photocredits: Abbreviations: l-left, r-right, b-bottom, t-top, c-centre, m-middle.
Front Cover —azure1. 1 – azure1. 2 – Krasowit. 3t – Olga Popova, 3m – jassada watt_, 3b – azure1. 4l – Oksana Kuzmina, 4m – studioloco, 4r – Ljupco Smokovski. 5t – HUANG Zheng, 5b – EpicStockMedia. 6 – Vasik Olga. 7 – BMJ. 8 – By E. Peter Steenstra/U. S. Fish and Wildlife Service - Northeast Region (Flickr) [Public domain or Public domain], via Wikimedia Commons. 9 – By OpenCage (http://opencage.info/pics/large_1141.asp) [CC BY-SA 2.5 (http://creativecommons.org/licenses/by-sa/2.5)], via Wikimedia Commons. 10 – JoeZ. 11t – CK Foto, 11b – You Touch Pix of EuToch. 12 – Dennis Jacobsen. 13 – PeterVandenbelt. 14 – By U.S. Fish and Wildlife Service Northeast Region (Atlantic Salmon Pre-Smolt) [CC BY 2.0 (http://creativecommons.org/licenses/by/2.0) or Public domain], via Wikimedia Commons. 15 – Konstantin Novikov. 16 – karamysh. 17 – Sekar B 18 – M.Khebra. 19 – Simon Tang. 20 – Hennadii H. 21 – Krasowit. 22t – Birdiegal, 22l – InsectWorld, 22b – Johnny Adolphson, 22r – Iv Mirin. 23 – Halfpoint. Images are courtesy of Shutterstock.com. With thanks to Getty Images, Thinkstock Photo and iStockphoto.